EARTH

Troll Associates

EARTH

by Keith Brandt

Illustrated by John Jones

Troll Associates

Library of Congress Cataloging in Publication Data

Brandt, Keith, (date)
  Earth.

  Summary: Describes the earth's physical characteristics,
its inner composition, and the changes that are constantly
taking place.
    1. Earth sciences—Juvenile literature. [1. Earth
sciences] I. Jones, John Ralph, 1935-   ill.
II. Title.
QE29.B694   1984   550   84-8444
ISBN 0-8167-0250-0 (lib. bdg.)
ISBN 0-8167-0251-9 (pbk.)

Our Earth is an exciting place. There are mountains that soar so high their snow-covered peaks pierce the clouds, and there are valleys that are green and rich with growing plants.

There is water everywhere—rivers snaking through canyons, vast oceans reaching from the shores of one continent to another, lakes and streams and waterfalls.

There are deserts, dry and barren. Volcanoes, glaciers, caves, beaches, rocky cliffs—our Earth has an endless variety of shapes and places.

Pluto

Uranus

The study of this fantastic planet is called *geology*. This name comes from the Greek word *ge* meaning "earth." Geologists are scientists who learn the story of our ever-changing Earth by studying such things as rocks, riverbeds, mountains, and volcanoes.

How did our planet come to be? Many billions of years ago, a vast cloud of gas swirled in space. Most of this gas became the

sun. But some of this gas became the nine planets of the solar system. One of them was our Earth, the third planet from the sun.

The Earth—a ball slightly flattened out at the poles—began its endless orbit 93 million miles from the sun. It also began its spin, or rotation, that makes day and night. In time, the planet developed an atmosphere. Water covered much of the Earth's surface.

13

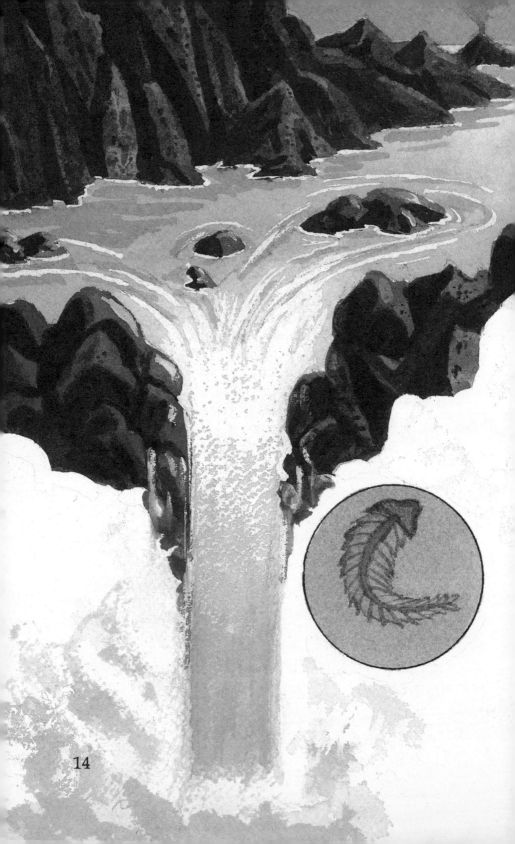

In the billions of years since our planet was formed, it has undergone many changes. Mountains have pushed up where oceans once covered the land. Deep canyons have been carved by wind and water. Volcanoes have created islands in one place, destroyed them in another.

Geologists believe that our ever-changing Earth is between four and five billion years old. They can tell this from the amount of radioactive substances, like uranium, that are found in rocks.

The oldest rocks on Earth date from the Precambrian Era. During this time the continents and oceans began to take shape. Simple forms of sea life appeared. Mountains began to rise. And huge glaciers covered much of the land.

Geologists call the next era the Paleozoic. It began about 600 million years ago and lasted about 350 million years. During the Paleozoic Era, the first fish appeared in the seas. Plants and swamp-like forests appeared on the land.

Then came the first insects, amphibians, and reptiles. Fossil fuels, such as coal, gas, and oil began to form from thick layers of plant and animal remains. Great floods covered much of North America.

Next came the Mesozoic Era, which lasted about 100 million years. During this era, dinosaurs roamed the world, then became extinct. This was also the era during which the first birds and mammals appeared.

The next era was the Cenozoic. This began 65 million years ago and is still going on. The world evolved into what it is today during the Cenozoic Era.

Many of the mammals we know—such as elephants, horses, apes, camels and rhinoceroses, and the ancestors of human beings—appeared during this time.

Less than two million years ago, during the Ice Age, huge glaciers covered large areas of North America and Europe. Then, as the ice retreated, the climate, geography, plant, and animal life began to change into what they are now.

Much of Earth's surface—about 70 percent—is covered by water. This includes all the ponds, lakes, streams, rivers, and oceans. The rest is dry land.

But the exact amounts and positions of the land masses and water areas are always moving and changing. This is because our Earth is not a cold, dead planet. It is a living, changing one.

When Earth first formed, and its surface cooled, the inside stayed hot. And it is still hot. Scientists believe the very center, which is called the inner core, consists of solid iron and nickel.

Outer
Core

Inner
Core

Mantle

The outer core, which surrounds the inner core, is so hot that the hardest metals are molten liquid.

Around the outer core is the mantle. The mantle, which is almost 2,000 miles thick, surrounds the core the way the fruit of a peach surrounds its pit. The mantle is also very hot, but not as hot as the core.

On top of the mantle is the thin layer that makes up Earth's surface, or crust. In some places this crust is only about five miles thick. And at other places, it is about twenty-five miles thick. This crust is not a solid skin, like the skin covering a peach. Instead, it is made up of separate masses of rock, called plates.

Plates

Mantle

These plates are very large. For example, the North American plate stretches from the middle of the Atlantic Ocean all the way across North America to the west coast. And

Pacific
Plate

North
American
Plate

the Pacific plate reaches from the west coast
of North America across the entire Pacific
Ocean to Japan.

Pacifi
Plate

All the plates are slowly moving. Where they meet, any of several things can happen. If two plates are moving toward each other, one plate may turn down, pushing the other one up and forming mountains.

If neither plate turns down, they may collide head-on, creating folded mountains, and crunching the Earth's surface like an accordion.

Or the two plates may not be headed for a head-on collision—instead, they may simply glance off one another, rubbing edges as they slip and slide past. A break in the Earth, called a *fault*, may mark the place where two plates are glancing off like this. The San Andreas Fault in California marks the place where the Pacific plate is moving north, past the North American plate.

Earthquakes and volcanoes can occur where two plates meet. That is why there have been many earthquakes along the west coast of North America and in Japan.

Mount Saint Helens, in the state of Washington, is a volcano that began erupting again in 1980, after a long period of inactivity. It is located near the edge of the North American plate.

As plates shift, other forces are also at work. Wind, rain, streams, rivers, oceans, and huge, moving glaciers change the world's surface. Sand, soil, and bits of rock are carried from place to place and deposited in layers, one on top of another.

These layers, called strata, build up over a long time and become sedimentary rock. Sandstone, shale, and coal are three kinds of sedimentary rock.

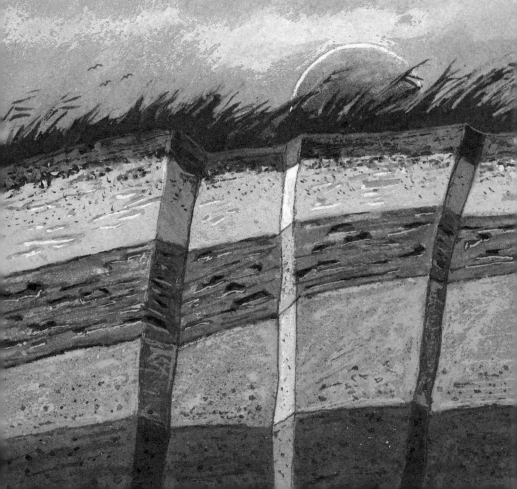

Granite

Basalt

Marble

Slate

Igneous rock is formed when molten rock material, called magma, cools and hardens deep within the Earth. Granite and basalt are two kinds of igneous rock.

Metamorphic rock was once igneous or sedimentary, until high temperatures and great pressures caused a change, or metamorphosis. Slate and marble are two kinds of metamorphic rock.

Geologists can tell the age of a mountain range by the kinds of rock it contains. Some mountains are made of many layers of sediment built up over millions of years. Some are the result of volcanic action. Some mountains are caused by shifts of Earth's crust along a fault line.

Older mountains have been worn and rounded by millions of years of wind and rain. Newer mountains are jagged and rough looking.

Someday these young mountains will be old, too, but more new mountains will thrust their peaks into the clouds.

Some volcanoes will die, others will burst forth. That is the fascinating story of our Earth. It is a story that has been going on for billions of years. And it will continue to unfold, year after year, century after century, because our Earth is not a cold, dead planet. It is a living, constantly changing one.